CREATURES
Of The Night

Horror Coloring Book

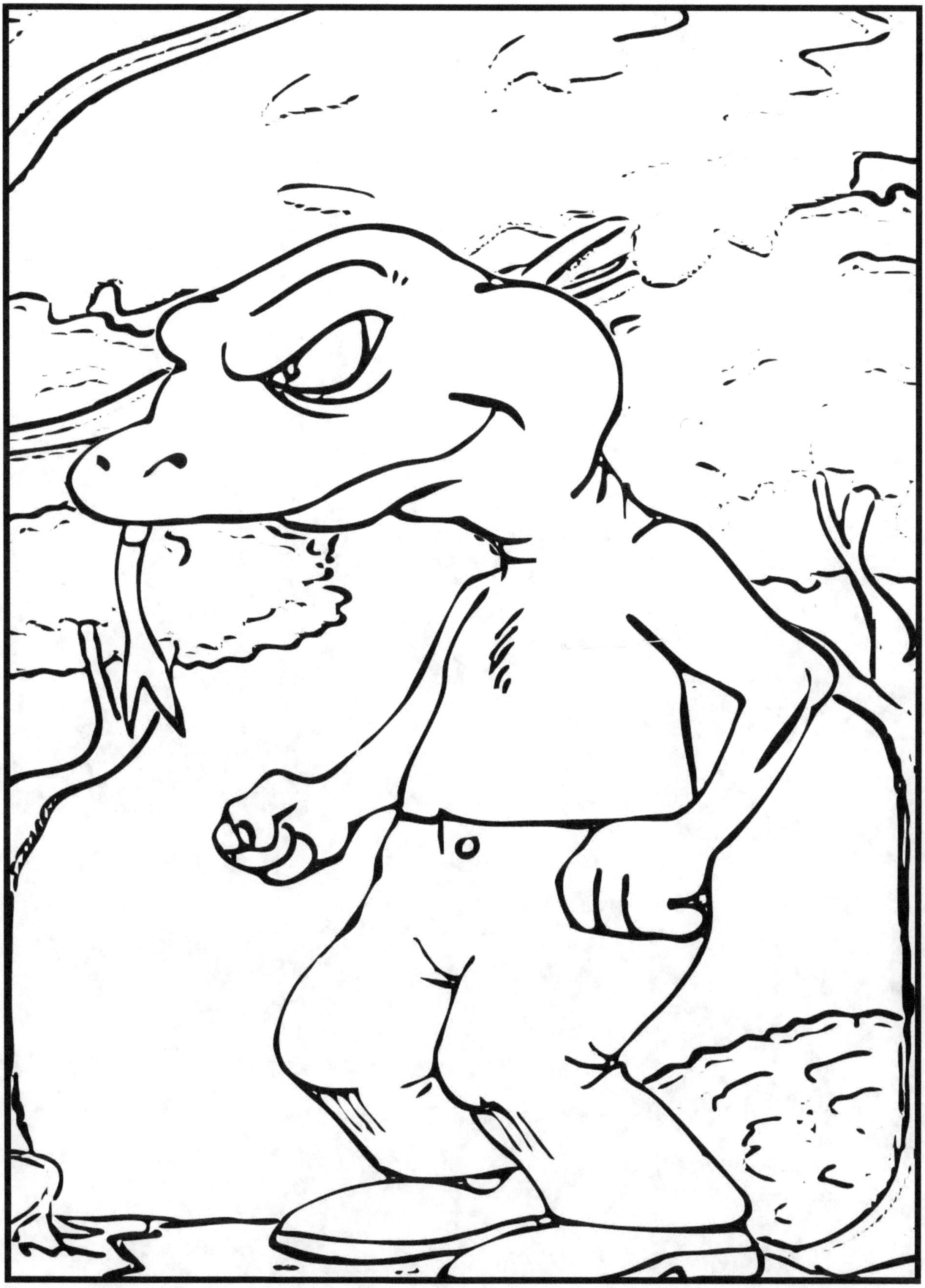

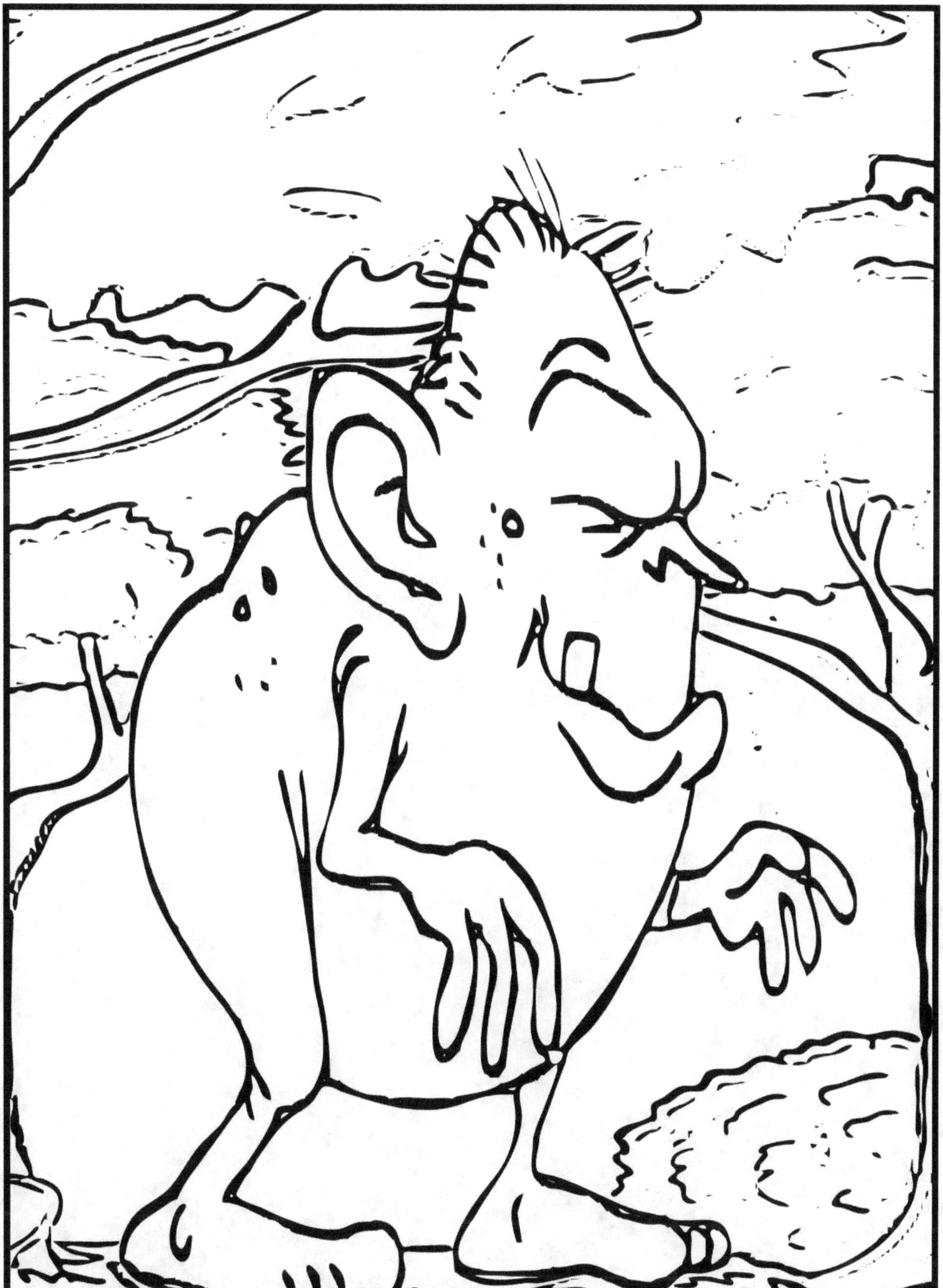

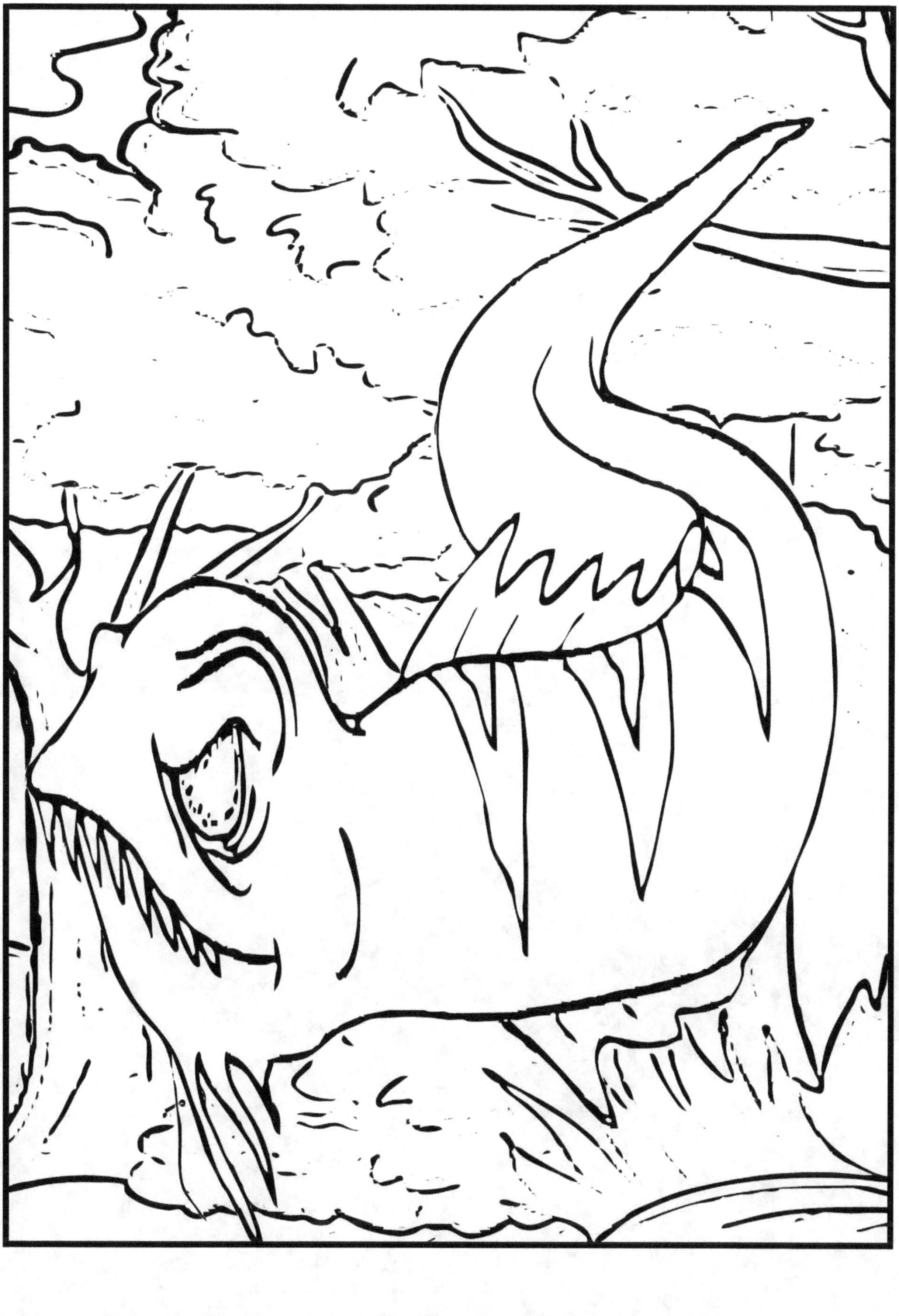

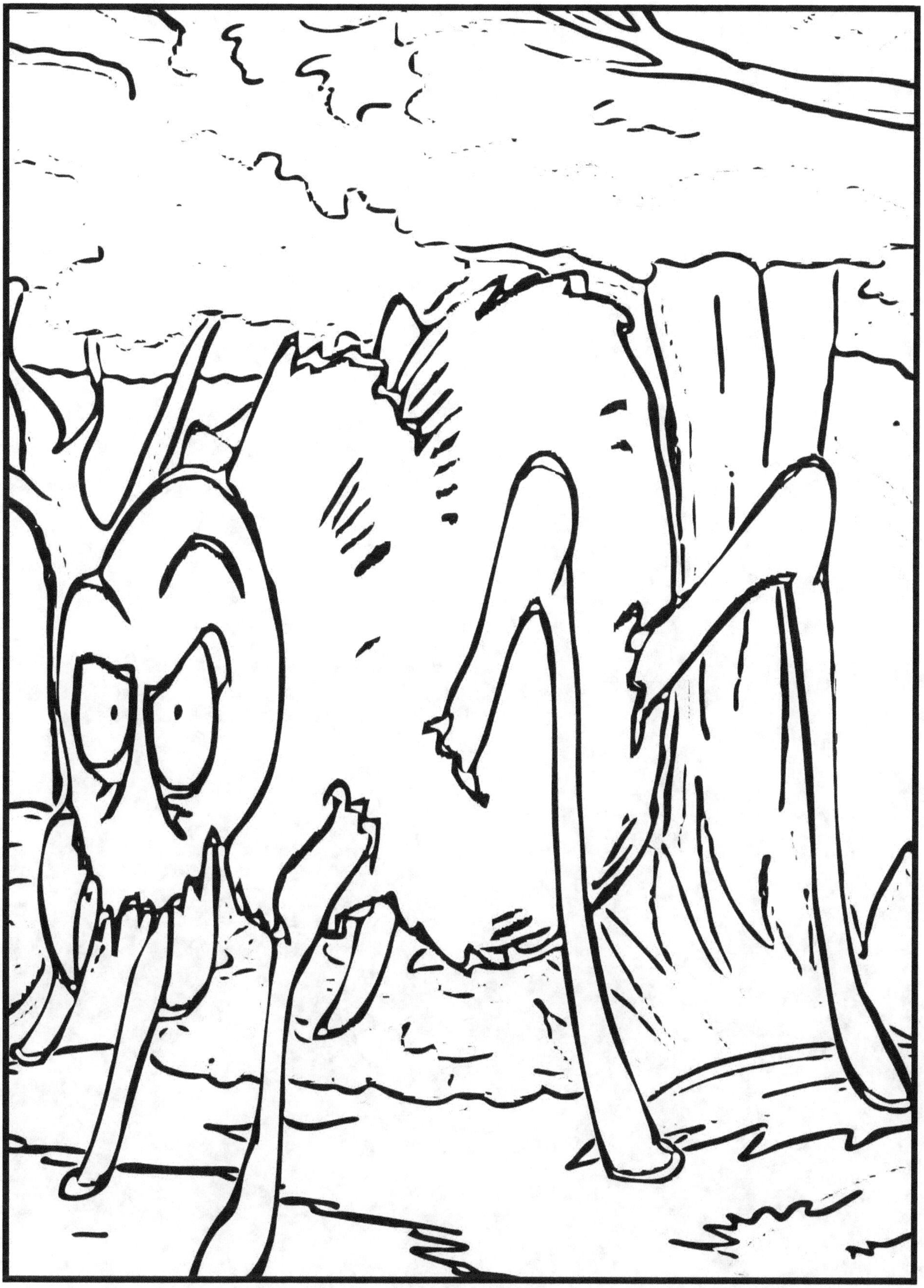

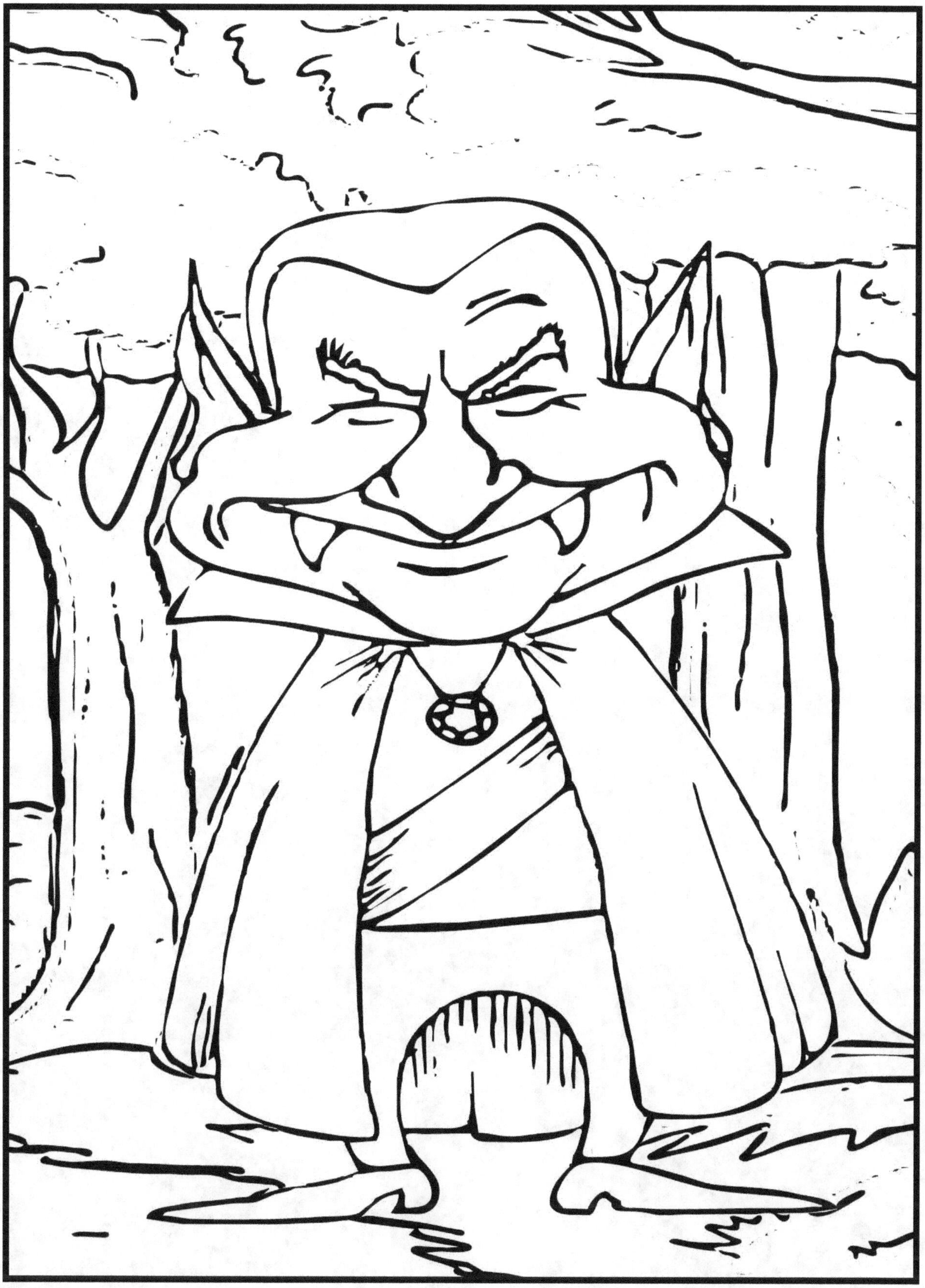

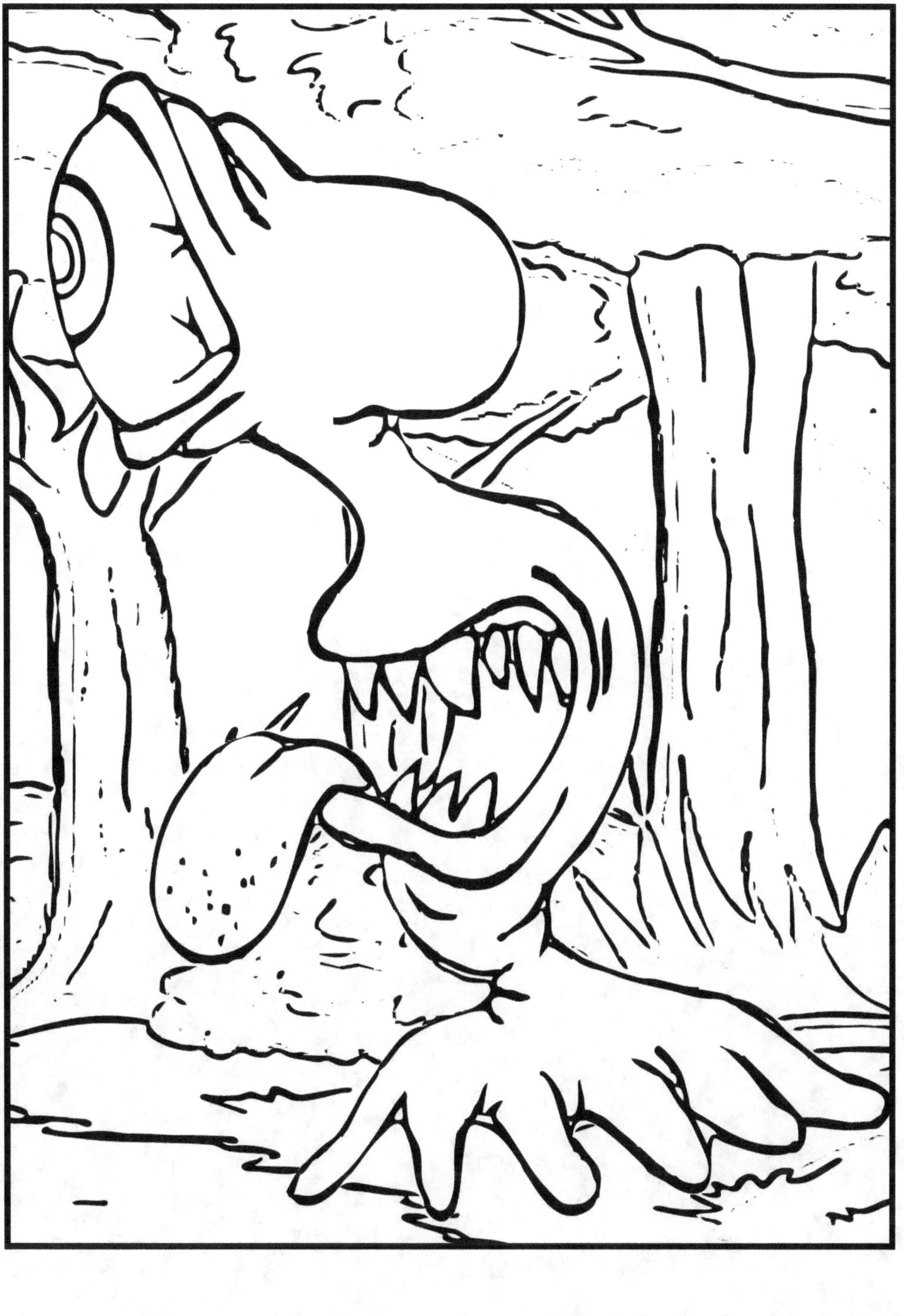

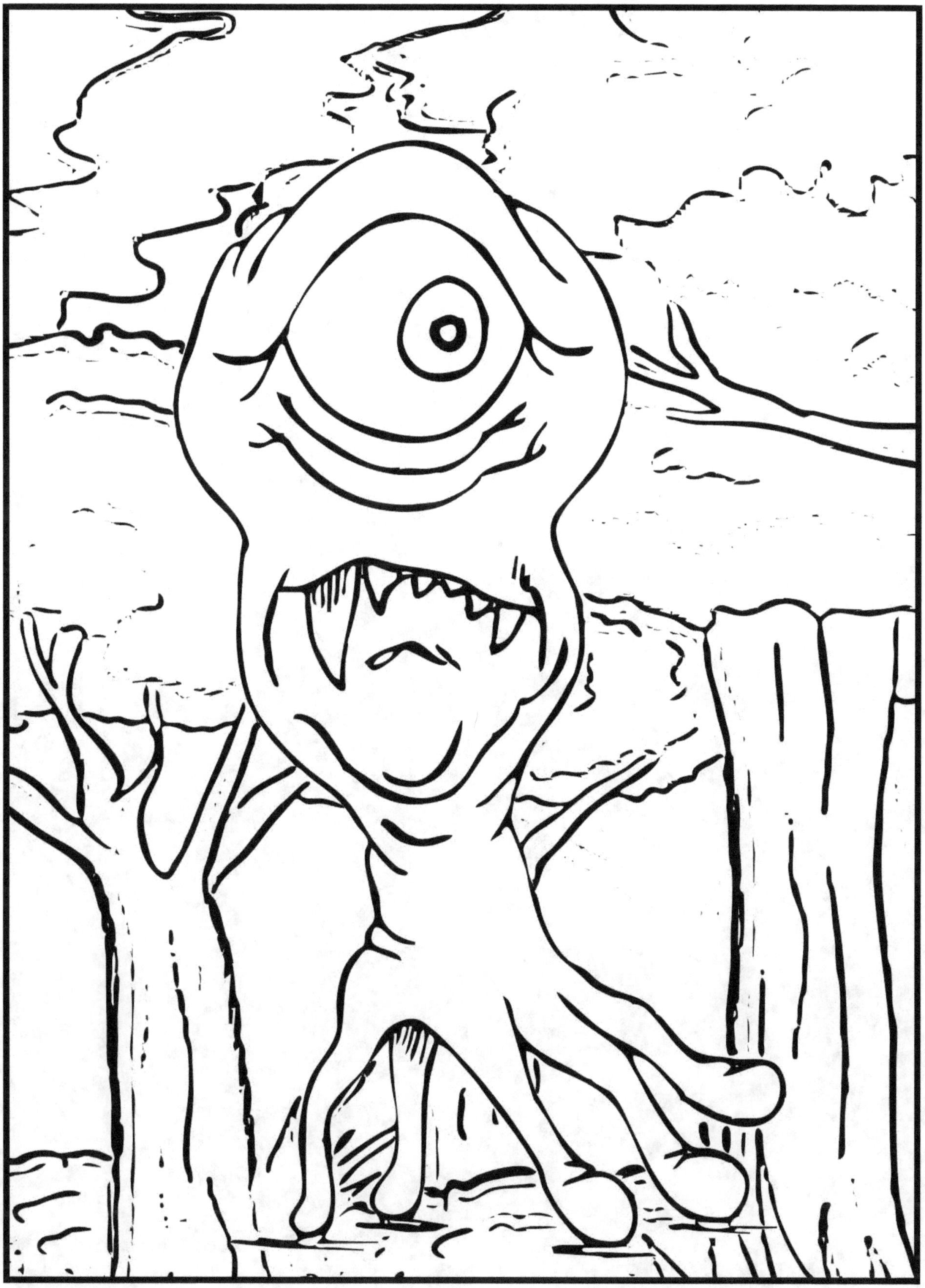

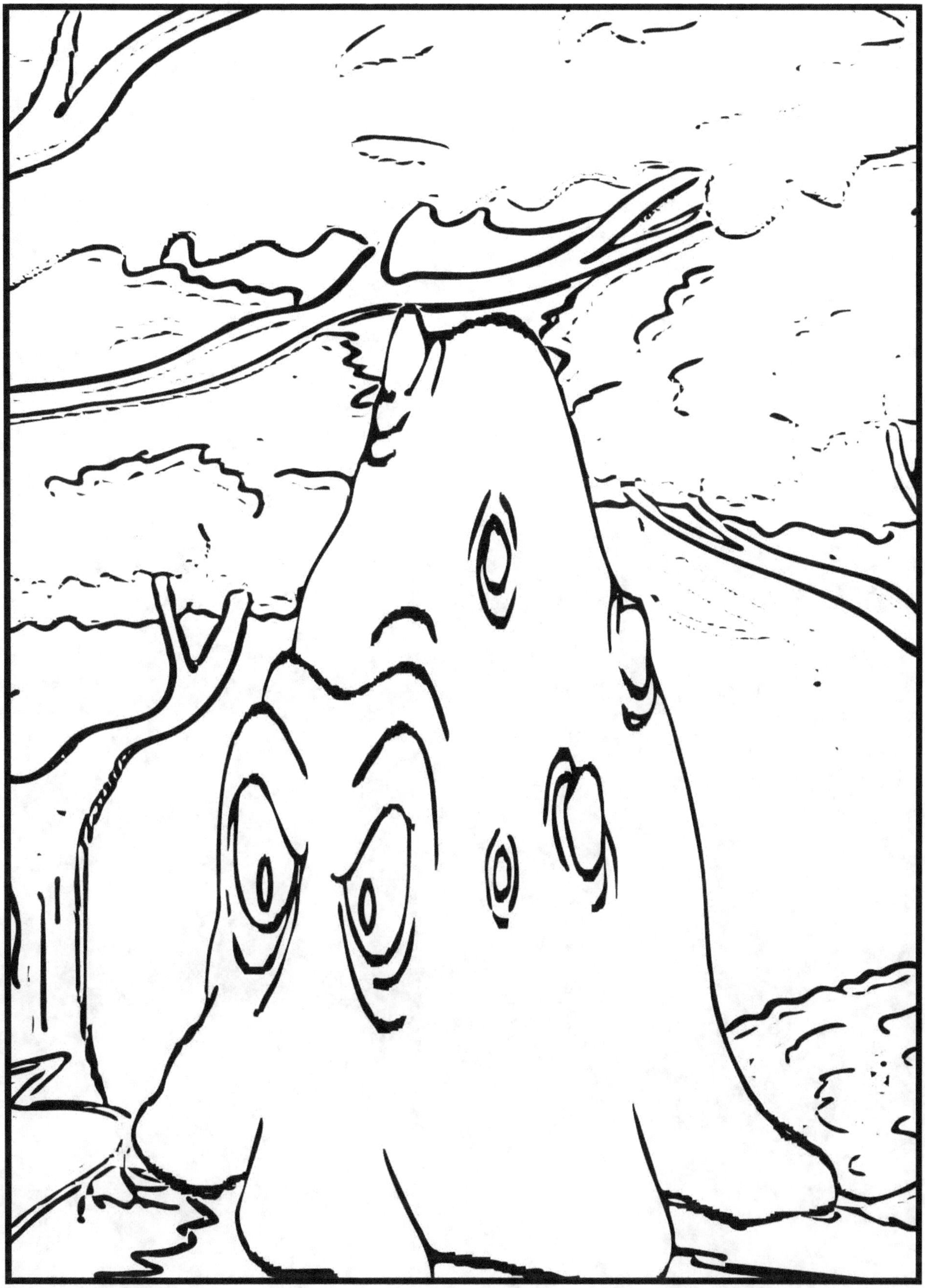

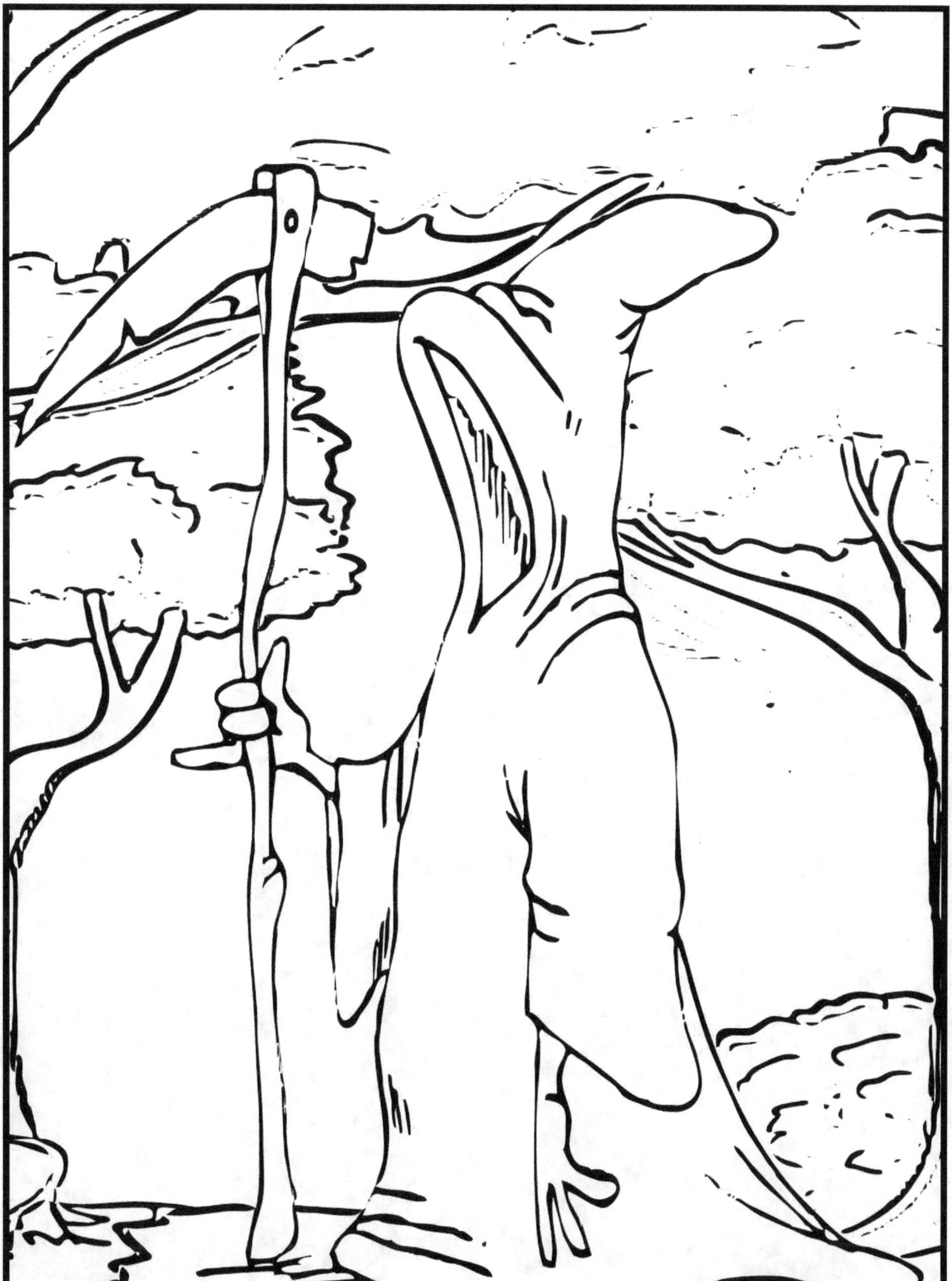

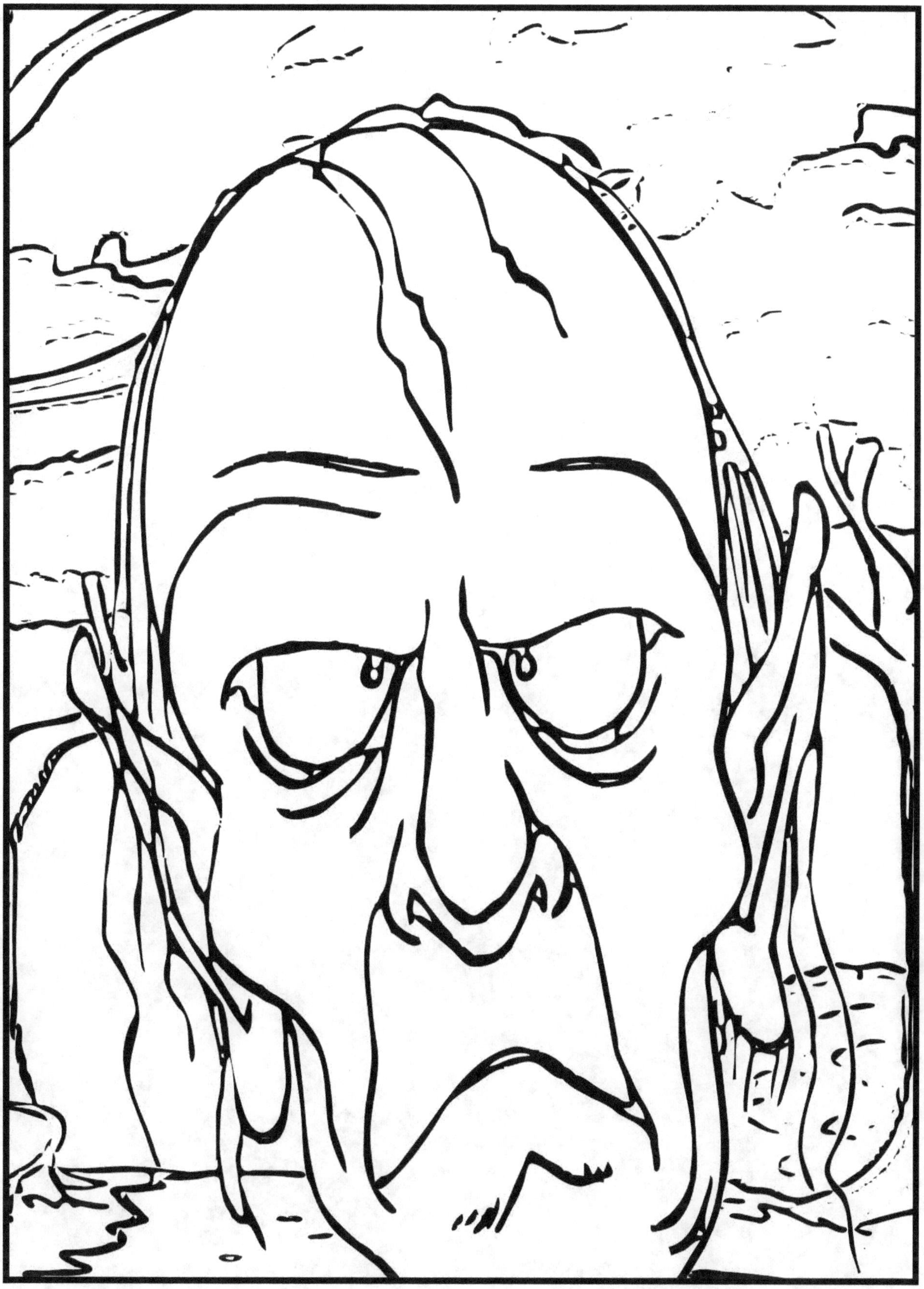

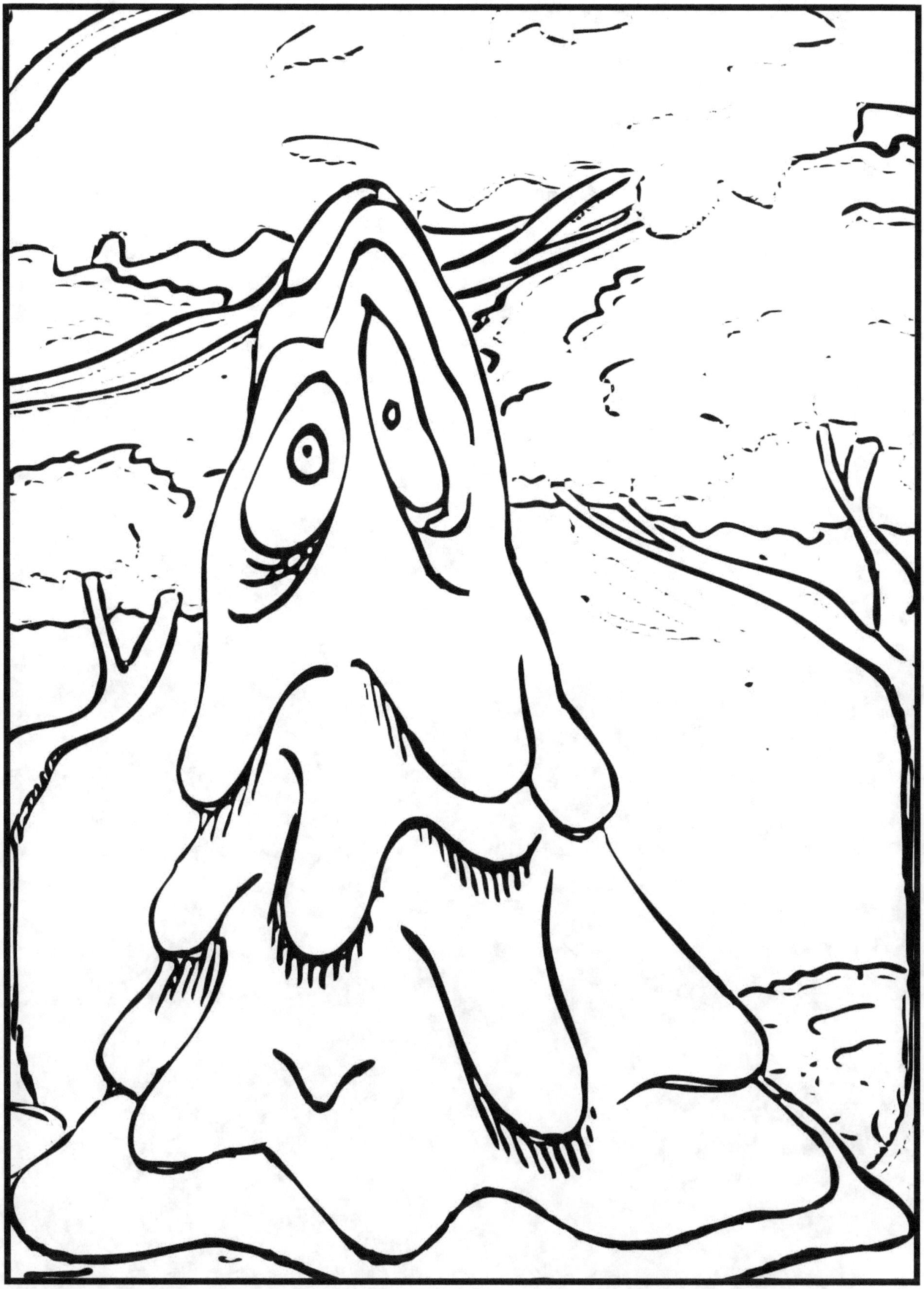

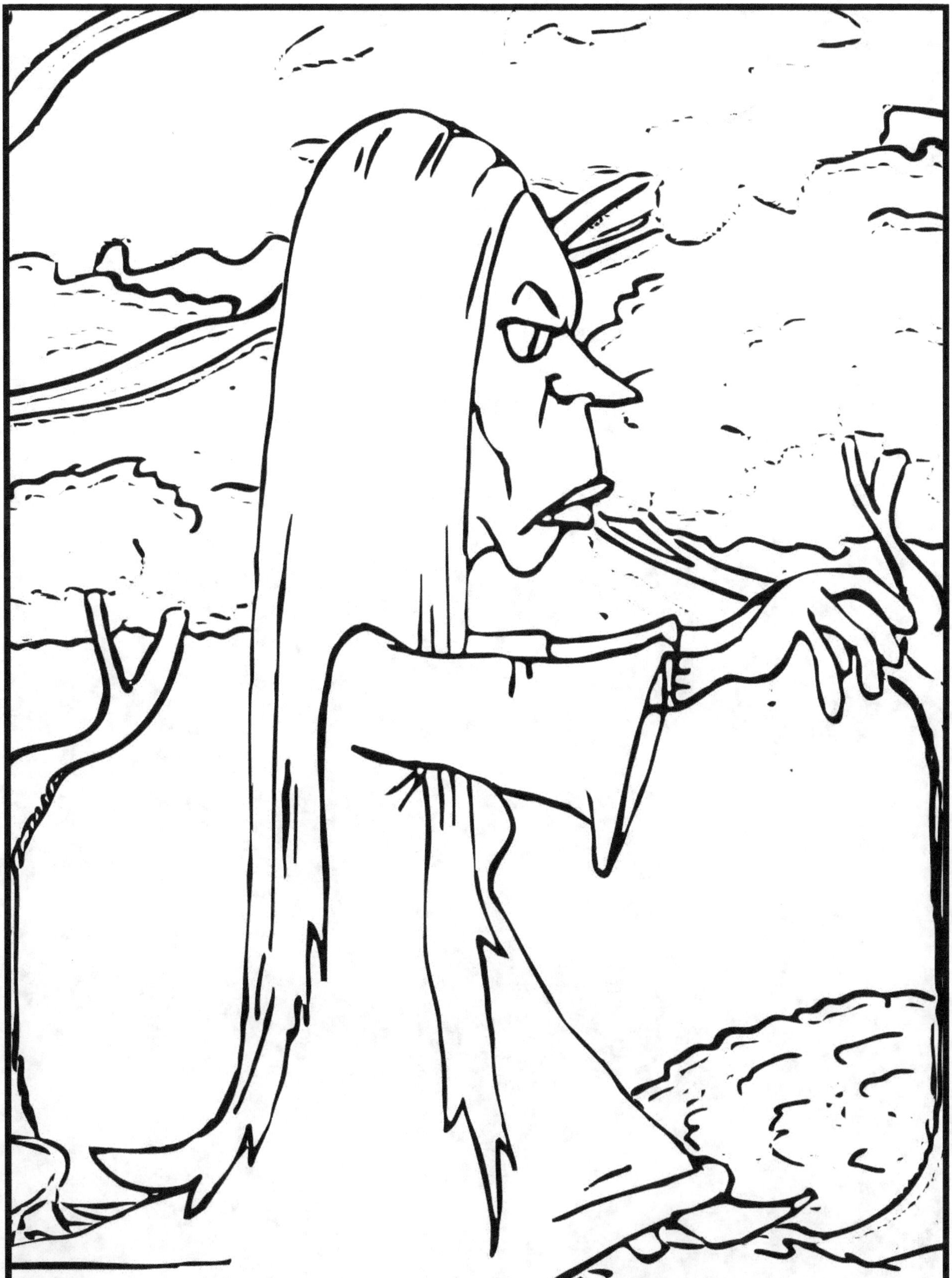

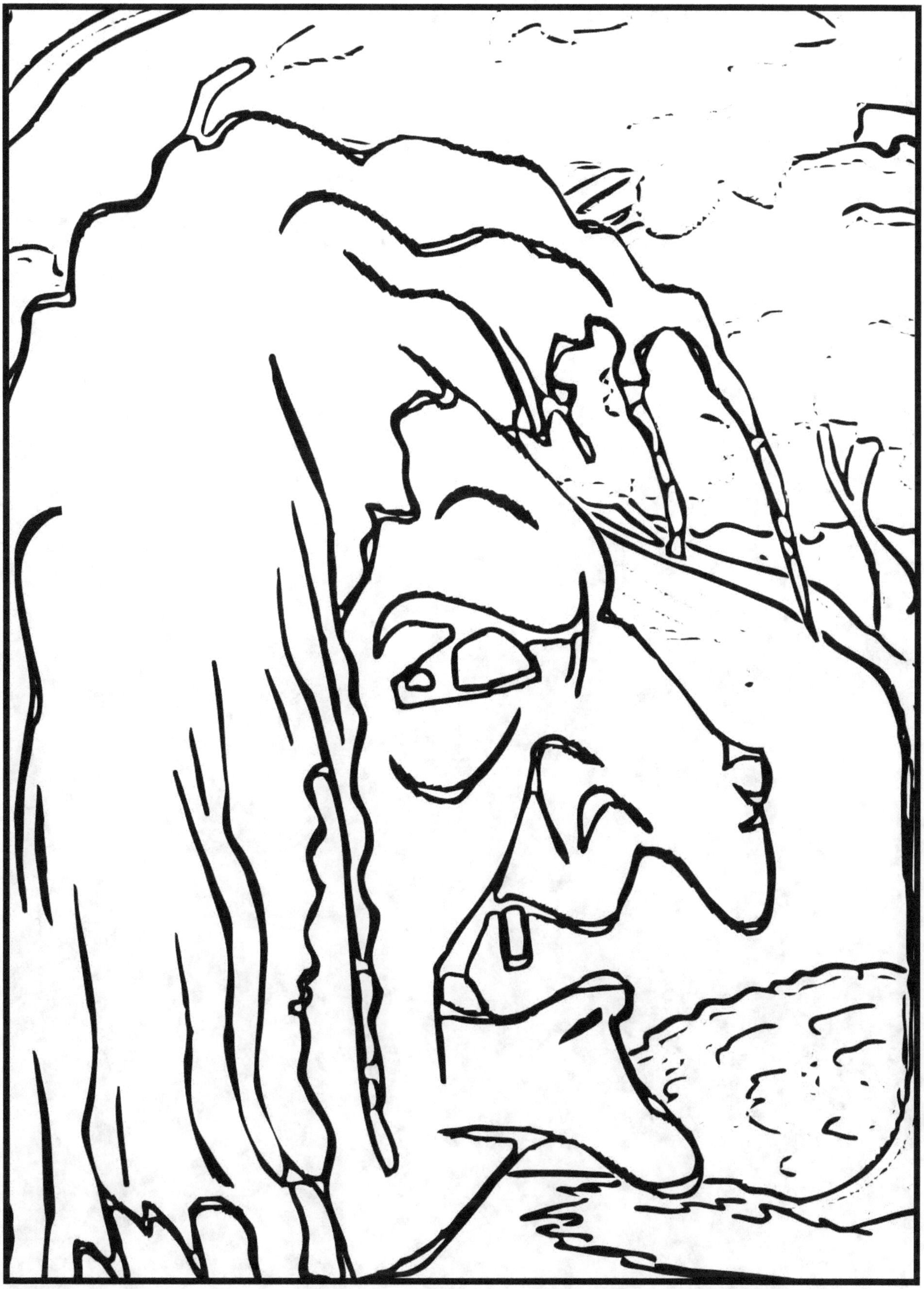

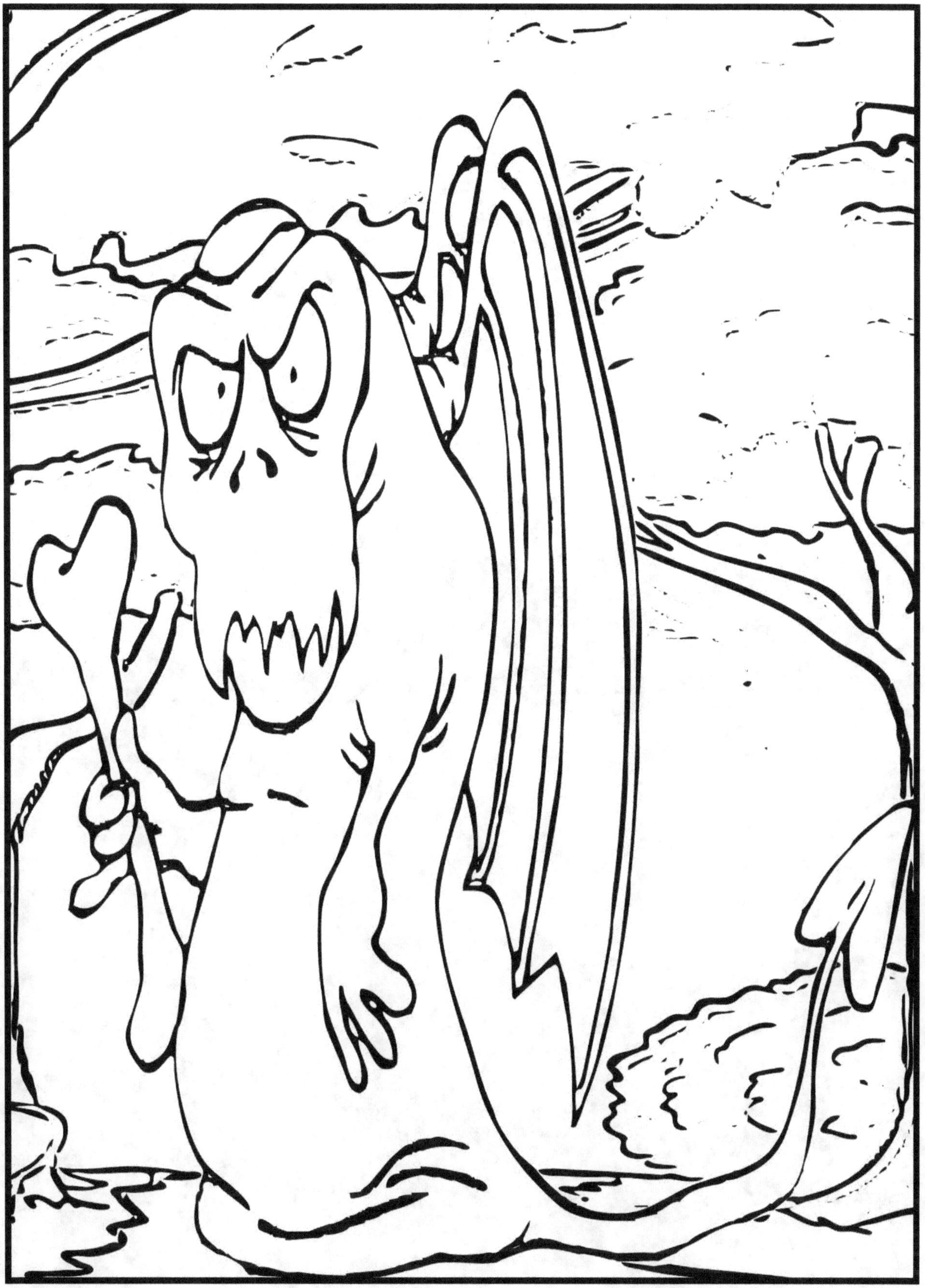

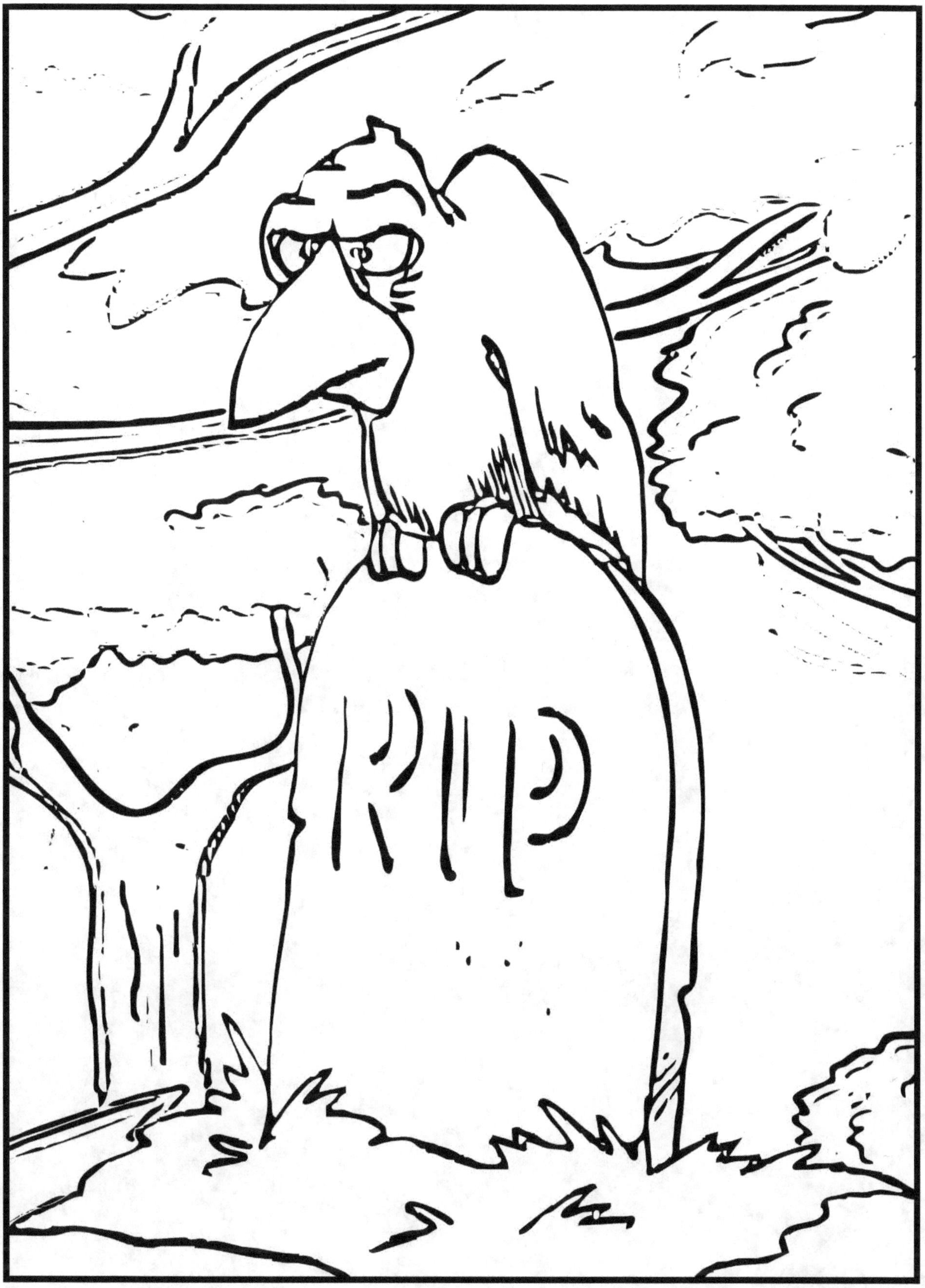
RIP

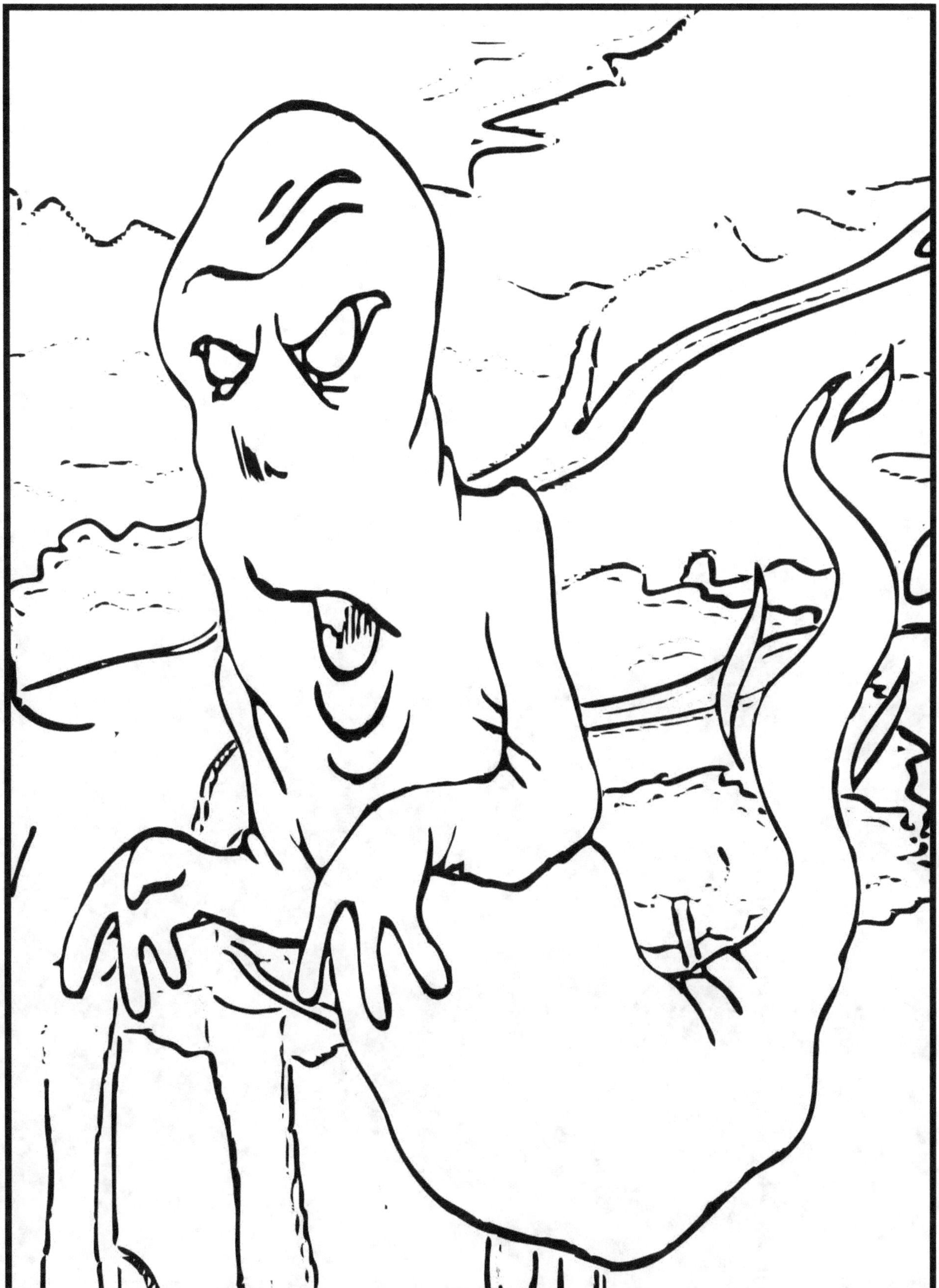

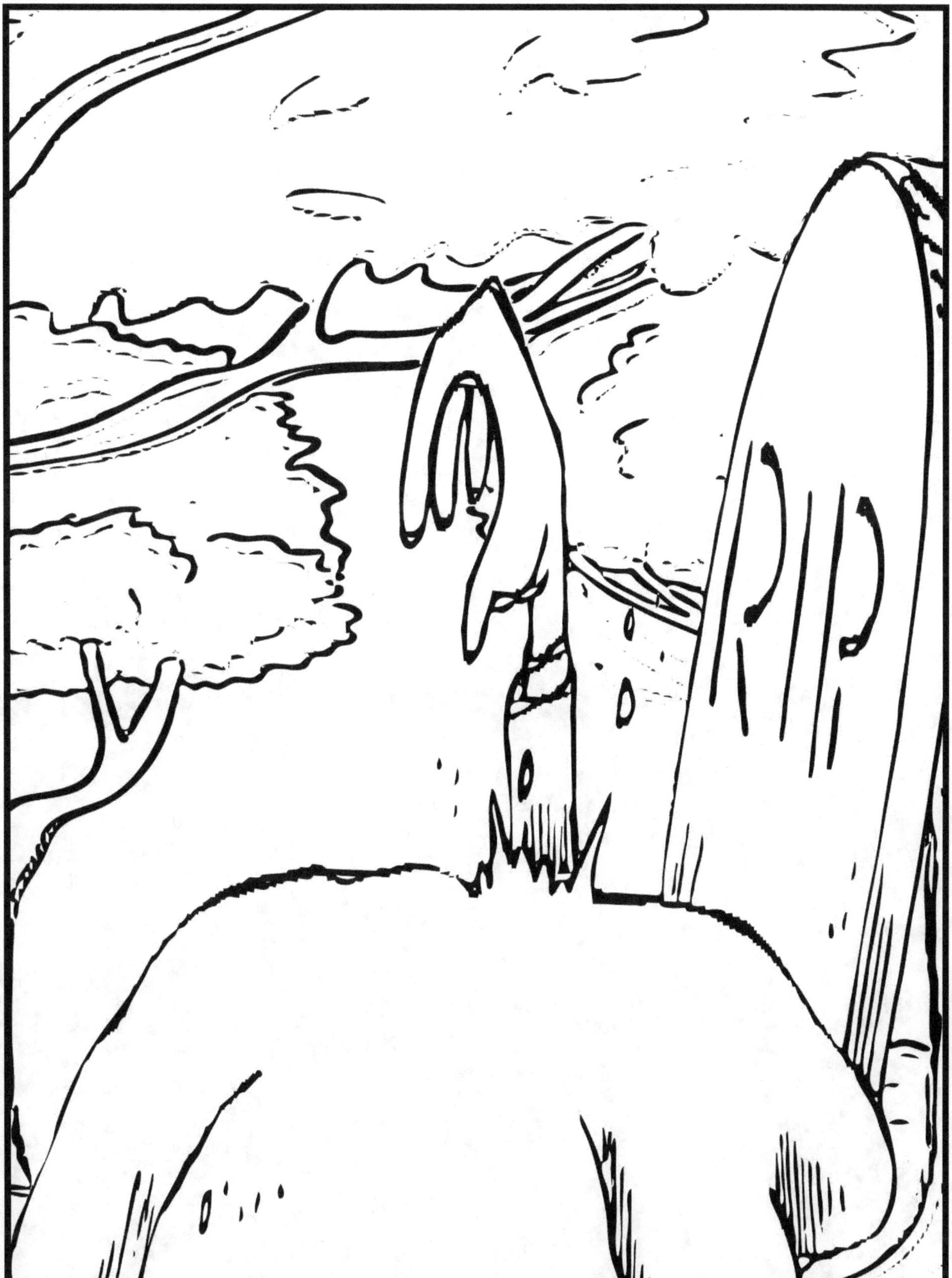
RIP

www.ingramcontent.com/pod-product-compliance
Lightning Source LLC
Chambersburg PA
CBHW081408170526
45166CB00010B/3261
* 9 7 8 1 5 1 9 7 7 5 4 1 2 *